# Win-win Philanthropy

## How <u>donor</u> and <u>donees</u> can achieve their goals simultaneously!

By

Robert J. Zimmerman, MBA, CFP

# INTRODUCTION

In the final decade of the 20th century, there appeared a news item in one of the Detroit papers that announced that a local billionaire had made arrangements to leave his entire estate to a local church organization. Subsequently, there was a letter to the editor entitled "You can be like M____".

The observation she made was: "Think about what local charities could accomplish if they had plenty of money to fulfill their visions. It just doesn't happen because people are uninformed". She continues: "Every person can choose who will spend their tax dollars. By default, their money leaves the area and goes to Uncle Sam, who distributes the money as the government sees fit."

That letter to the editor is the inspiration for this book. Many homes haves a library of recipe books, but few have a guide for gifting. Years of exposure to the financial scene has generated a large amount of financial observation. That body of knowledge has enabled development of a sizable 'recipe' book of financial planning ideas. These ideas are available to all those who would like to be a 'hero' to some worthwhile charitable cause.

As the lady states in her observation: "In philanthropy, everybody wins. The donors have more money as long as one of two spouses is alive, heirs can actually receive a large inheritance, and your favorite charities typically end up with more money that would have gone to Uncle Sam. It's a win-win situation".

In the particular case of the industrialist that made the news, it was never disclosed what arrangements were finalized, but it is not likely that he intended to disinherit his family. Guided by his planner, he could have left them with the same amount they would have received after paying the taxes on his estate. Plus, he could have enjoyed tax benefits during his own lifetime.

Whenever we receive a solicitation for funds from some charity, we are reminded of the statement she made that people are uninformed. We would love to be able to provide financial sustenance for a great number of worthwhile causes, but, financially, this is not realistic. However, we can do something by showing 'others' how they can do far more than they ever thought they could - by simply becoming more informed. That is what this book is intended to do.

There will be two sections to this book. Recognizing the basic fact that charities have immediate needs for funding, the first will deal with right now gifting, and the second will be a section dealing with long term planning for those who listen to the words of Kahlil Gibran:

"Give now, while the season of giving is yours, and not your inheritors".

Many established charities offer gift annuities, but that is about as close to discussing insurance contracts as they care to come. As a result, this planning tool is usually greatly underutilized. Here, we will talk about many creative uses for insurance contracts that allow for increased revenue to charities while simultaneously advancing the financial goals of the donors. In other words, we seek to identify some 'win-win' situations as implored by the lady who wrote the letter to the editor in the 1990's.

A charitable mindset is the only ingredient in every recipe for helping charity that cannot be eliminated. Without that frame of mind, nothing we can offer here will make any difference. If you are one who is open to learning more, we think you will find in this recipe book of ideas one that may suit your appetite.

In the minds of most people, giving to a charity is a 'sacrifice' that abandons a current use of the funds donated entirely. A dime left

3

in the 'March of dimes' canister is a dime that could feed a parking meter. A five dollar bill in the collection plate at church could buy a burger or two at McDonalds, and so on. That is obviously true, but it ignores the immediate psychological payoff of supporting a worthy cause, and the fact that it is possible many times to help others while meeting your own goals at the same time.

When we observe a large turnout for a charitable walk or other local event, and when we observe the ongoing success of the Salvation Army, the Red Cross, and so many other ongoing charities, it serves to confirm that there is still a willingness to make an effort to support worthwhile causes and thereby have an impact beyond meeting the basic human needs for personal survival.

Most importantly, it does not require a millionaire to be a 'hero' to charity. You will see many situations where a person of modest means can have an impact. If just one idea fits your particular situation, we think the effort to assemble this book will be justified. If you do have the inclination to be a help financially to your neighbor, we offer out congratulations and hope this book will be of value to you.

# Table of Contents

Part One – WinWin Today

## Examples

| | | |
|---|---|---|
| 1. | Martha, at 85, needed more income. | 8 |
| 2. | Harry had an offer on his real estate holding, but there was a tax problem. | 9 |
| 3. | Mary only had $25,000, but - | 10 |
| 4. | Larry converted a tax bill into a tax deduction | 12 |
| 5. | Max and Marianne liked the gift annuity, but - | 13 |
| 6. | Marion forgot to remember them in her will. | 15 |
| 7. | Ron and Rita like to travel, and they also like dogs. | 16 |
| 8. | Linda was worried that her home care fund would run out. | 18 |
| 9. | Leonard was tired of paying for health insurance. | 19 |
| 10. | Harriet was scrimping along because of low interest rates at the bank. | 21 |
| | Part Two – Win-Win Tomorrow | 23 |

## Examples

| | | |
|---|---|---|
| 1. | Sally had a nice real estate investment to sell. | 24 |

2.      Frank was able to give his estate away twice.          26

3.      Ken wasn't sure when to retire.          27

4.      Jerry had group life insurance that was expiring.          28

5.      Gloria did not need the RMD that she was required
        to take every year.          30

6.      John tripled the size of his grandchildren's
        educational fund.          31

7.      Mark used an unneeded IRA distribution to help
        the church, plus -          33

8.      Tony wanted to win back the stock market losses
        in his 401k account.          34

9.      Jim and Jenny wanted to pass to their children
        the IRA account tax free.          36

10.     Dorothy wanted to help her church but did not
        want to disinherit her children.          37

                Epilogue          39

# PART ONE

## Win-Win Today

Charities are constantly seeking revenues from their donor base in order to support the financial needs of their mission.   Many do not have the luxury of enjoying a permanent financial base.  That is the reason you will be the recipient of constant pleas for support through the mail, and through the electronic media. Local charities rely on down to earth tactics, from bake sales to marathons to selling cookies – let your imagination run.

The result is they are not usually active in setting up long term planning to increase their financial base.  The extent of their advance planning is typically a plea to 'remember us in your will'.

Offsetting the needs of these charities are the needs of the potential donor.   While many everyday folks would like to respond to the pleas for help, there is only so much they can do. They have their own budgetary needs, and they are under the impression that they must compromise those needs in order to help out their favorite charity.

What if there was a way for the donors of the world to satisfy their own financial needs and help out charity at the same time. Would that not be a 'win-win' situation?   In this section, we will simply describe some situations in which those with a charitable mindset can help themselves while also benefiting a favorite charity.

These examples will all utilize the guarantee features available only from insurance contracts.  The term ' insurance contracts' includes both life insurance and annuities.  Each model is taken from an actual or theoretical real life situation, and is presented to open the mind of a potential donor who may find it practical to further investigate the potential for their own particular circumstance.

# MARTHA

In good health for her age, Martha was concerned that her bank savings account would run out if she used more than the meager interest rate she was receiving. Her $50,000 account was paying less than $500 a year, so if she took out anything over that, she would be using up her principal.

She really wanted to support her church, but her budget was strained already because of the low income from her savings account. Her son was aware of her situation, and talked to his adviser. The adviser pointed out how Martha could help her church while increasing her income at the same time.

By moving the account to a reputable insurance company, she could immediately give her church a donation of $2,500, and she could still enjoy an annual income of almost $3,600. That $300 a month added to her budget made a big difference to her daily enjoyment of life. But even more so, she appreciated the fact that she never need to worry about running out of money, even if she lived another 25 years.

The account with the insurance company could possibly have a balance remaining in it at the time of her passing. She could leave that to her church or to her son, but that was a choice she could decide on at any time. For the time being, she elected to leave it to the church, with her son's approval. Her church was very appreciative of the immediate donation, as well as the potential future legacy. For Martha, and for her church, it was truly a 'win-win' plan.

(This example simply points out that it is now possible to obtain a guaranteed income for life without giving up any control over the ultimate destiny of the funds. A traditional 'life' annuity leaves behind any unused funds to the insurance company. Modern contracts do not demand that the client give up control of their account in order to enjoy a lifetime income guaranty. Martha was able to increase the return on her savings to over 7%, even after making an immediate donation to her church.)

## HARRY

The building that had been the home of his business for so many years had gone through a tough era due to the changing nature of the city. Located on a main thoroughfare in the city, the values had seen a very dry period of time when it was in doubt that anyone would be willing to buy the property when Harry wanted to retire.

He had a very low cost basis in the property, but even then, he would have had a capital gains tax to pay if he were able to find a willing seller. So he merely held on, finding an occasional tenant, and occupying a part of the building to house his remaining business interests.

Then the news came out that a major development would be taking place on the land adjacent to his building. When that finally came about, his building was of significant value, and behold - he had an offer to buy it for $550,000. He was mulling it over due to the high tax bill it would give him, and while he was thinking about it, the offer was increased to $600,000.

Harry had never been one to pay high taxes, and this problem was one that went directly counter to his instinct. He was a graduate of the local university, and was aware of their tax relief program which he understood would help him manage his tax bill, while at the same time providing a significant benefit to his alma mater. He asked them to run the numbers for him.

What Harry found was that he could arrange for the school to receive title to the property, and they would then become the seller. In exchange, they would give him a lifetime income for as long as he lived. Instead of having a big tax bill to pay, he would receive a charitable income tax deduction of over $140,000 which could be spread over future years if not needed in the current tax year. So instead of having a large tax bill, he received a very nice tax credit. He was happy that he listened.

Harry would receive nearly $23,000 every year which would include some of the capital gains from the increased value realized on the sale, but that would be offset by the tax deduction that was left over. Harry wanted the income to last over his life and his wife's life. However, he named his son as the joint recipient with the understanding that his son would use the funds to support his mother if needed, and would then be entitled to the income for as long as he lived.

(This is an example of how a gift annuity program works to provide an income stream for a donor. There are a variety of ways to use the income that   In this case, there was an immediate benefit for the donor, and the charity realized nearly $300,000 to fund their needs. This was truly a win-win situation for the immediate benefit of both parties.
(If Harry was not in need of the income immediately, he could have followed the example of Sally elsewhere in this book and used the income to purchase a paid up insurance policy. At his age, 75, and In spite of issues with elevated book pressure, he could have obtained nearly $120,000 of life insurance that would be fully paid for in 5 years. That amount would have become available to him while living if his health changed and he needed money for professional health care.   After 5 years, the income would be paid to him or his son for as long as either lived.)


## MARY

Every time she watched those ads on TV asking for $19 a month, Mary felt as if they were causes for which she was emotionally inclined to commit. However, she only had $25,000 life savings in the bank, and she wanted to leave that money to her daughter. After all, by living with her daughter, she was able to get by on her husbands pension plus her social security.

10

It bothered her that the bank account was paying such a low rate of interest, and she did not feel comfortable in committing $38 monthly to support her two favorite causes that she saw on those heart tugging television ads.

When her daughter's adviser visited the house one day, she was able to tell the adviser about her wishes and her limitations. Here is a plan the adviser suggested for her:

- Place $20,000 into an insurance account with a company he recommended
- Leave $5,000 in the bank account for emergency funds.
- Have the insurance company send her a check every month that would pay her a much higher income than she was receiving from the bank.
- Mary was 70 years old, and the insurance company committed to sending her $100 every month.
- This check would be sent to her as long as she lived, and would also provide for her daughter who was 45 to receive a check for her lifetime.

The check she received every month allowed her to send $19 every month to her five favorite causes, and she had money left over to put back into her bank account if she wished. Or, she could use the extra income to increase her contribution to her church.

(Unlike the traditional insurance payouts which she had been taught to avoid, she did not give up control of her account just because she took a guaranteed life time income. The money she was receiving every month was approximately 6% of her deposit, but the account was being credited with interest that was greater than that which the bank was able to pay, so her principal was able to be preserved to some extent. Plus, it meant something to her to know that her daughter would continue to receive a monthly check on the account after she passed on.)

# LARRY

At the age of 52, Larry had enjoyed a rewarding career in the field of information technology. Early in his career, he was able to invest in a technology company that proved to be a very successful investment. His $30,000 investment had grown in value to $92,500. Larry felt that this company had had its run and was likely to settle down as an average performer. Since it was not paying any dividends, it was basically a dormant asset.

On giving it some thought, he felt that the values might be better deployed elsewhere, but he knew that if he sold the investment, it would cause his current income tax bill to increase substantially. He was reluctant to do so, even though he felt the investment had its best days behind.

His wife, Linda, was happily seeing to the task of raising a family, while at the same time tending to the needs of her mother who was in failing health. There was a small amount of life insurance on her life, but nothing that would really help to replace her true economic value.

Larry took the opportunity to visit with a member of the stewardship committee at church to see if anything could be done to help the church while at the same time helping him the meet his own goals. He was told that in a similar situation there was a practical solution that made sense.

As a result of that conversation, Larry donated the stock to the church which they sold for $92,500, and in exchange, he received an annual check for the remainder of both his life and Linda's life. The check would be for $3,500 and it would last for as long as either of them lived.

So, instead of paying a tax on the capital gains of $62,500, Larry was able to take a tax credit that year for a charitable gift of over $17,000. Better yet, he was able to use that check every year to pay for life insurance for Linda, and that check would be there to pay the premiums as long as they lived.

For that annual premium, Linda was able to qualify for a life insurance plan in the amount of over $300,000. The really significant aspect of this plan was the benefit that allowed her to access up to $6,000 a month from the face amount if she were to be in need of long term care – either at home or in a facility.

When Larry made that stock investment a few years earlier, he certainly hoped it would be a good investment. It turned out much different than he expected when it not only allowed him to support a charity and help him with his income taxes, it provided a valuable source of security for his wife, with a growing account value that could be used for future tax free income if needed.

On taking a look at the potential earnings in the insurance account, Larry actually decided it would be better to use the insurance account than to contribute to a Roth IRA. Up to the limits that the law allowed, he put as much extra with the insurance as he could in order to allow him to have a future income tax free retirement supplement.

 (Larry not only solved the problem of paying a large tax bill for the current year, he made a significant contribution to charity. As a side effect, he filled a planning need for Linda's future financial security, all the while eliminating the question of finding money to make premium payments.)


## MAX and MARIANE

Like many retirees, Max and Marianne had saved for their retirement years, and they planned to use the interest from their savings to enhance their life style in the senior years.

When they finally retired, they found that the interest rates were so low that they could not use their savings without the fear of outliving the account. They had discussed it, and since part of their plan was to leave any remaining balance in their account to their favorite charity, they decided to look further into the offer of a gift annuity.

After realizing that the gift annuity meant abandoning control of the funds, they looked into an alternative that enabled them to support their charity and still increase their 'guaranteed lifetime income' that meant so much to their peace of mind. Here is what they did with a $100,000 CD that was expiring:

- They made a $5,000 donation to their charity
- They placed the remainder of the amount into a commercial annuity that provided immediate income fo life of over $5,000 a year.

Here is the result of that decision:

- Max's age was 75 and Marianne was 73. They could enjoy a $5300 check every year, the equivalent of a 5.3% interest yield on their expiring CD.
- The income was guaranteed to last as long as either of them lived
- The actual interest credited on the annuity was linked to a tock market index.
- The actual interest rate history on the account was impressive to him.
- He retained full control of the account.
- Any remaining balance in the account on death could go to his charity.

Max's decision was based on a thorough review of his overall finances with his adviser. He was gratified to see his donation at work in his charity, and even more so when he was able to enjoy a $5,000 deduction on the next year's tax returns.

( This is an example of how the need for a guaranteed income was met while still making an immediate contribution to charity. It satisfied an immediate goal, and potentially left a future legacy to their charity for any residual value in their annuity.)

## MARION

Whenever you see a reminder to 'remember us in your will' for a charity, it should remind you of the fact that the use of a will is not the best way to transfer an asset to your loved ones.

Most people do not realize that a will cannot go into effect until a probate court approves it. There are many attorneys who make their living by handling the probate process for those who chose to leave their assets to heirs with the planning tool known as a 'will'.

The need for such attorney is evident from the multitude of laws that govern transfer of title to heirs. In addition to the time delay typically involved in the probate process, there is always the potential for disputing the document. Plus the fact that the entire process is a matter of public record. So much for privacy! The point is that when you use a will, there is no way to avoid the laws of the state where property is located.

For those who prefer to avoid this process, there is a much more efficient way to handle things – use an insurance contract. You simply tell the insurance company where to send the check, and they follow your orders – absolutely no involvement with the probate system. This is true not only of life insurance policies, but also with annuities.

For those who pay attention to the 'remember us in your will' plea, here is an example of how you may benefit 'today' by helping charity at the same time:

Marion, age 60, wanted to leave $100,000 to charity as part of her legacy. She would have given the money right away, and taken a tax credit immediately. There were two problems, however. First, the tax credit did not help her because she was already in

15

such a low bracket that the credit meant little to her.  Second, she could not be sure that she would not need money for personal health care while she was living.  So she left the money in the bank, and at a low rate of interest it remained there with no effective increase in value.

She heard a friend talk about a single deposit insurance plan, and decided to investigate it.  She found that not only did it offer much higher interest rates than the bank account, but also it increased the amount that would be available to her if she needed money for health care while she was still living.

At her age, the $100,000 deposit was converted into a fully paid up insurance contract for $203000.  Since that amount would be available to her in full if she needed health care, there was an immediate benefit to her from knowing that there would be more available if she needed care in the future.  She also knew that she could have access to the funds if she needed them for other purposes, but she fully intended to simply let the insurance remain in full force.

(This example could belong in the 'tomorrow' part of the book, but it is placed here to demonstrate the 'right now' benefit to the donor in the form of increased peace of mind while living.  The mindset in favor of charity was always present, but the impact was increased by the step of moving her account to a more beneficial arrangement.
She named the charity as the beneficiary for any part of the face amount that was not needed for health care, and informed the charity that they would benefit in the future to the extent she remained healthy.)

## RON and RITA

At their ages of 65, Ron and Rita had discovered Elder Hostel programs several years ago.  These trips combined a variety of educational and recreational programs in various sites around the country, and they always found that it was a great way to meet new people. The programs typically lasted 5 to 7 days and cost between $1500 and $1,800 for a couple. The program name had been updated to 'Road Scholars', but the format had remained the same.

They had set aside a savings account specifically to allow them to select a program each year. That account was $30,000 and it was earning a very low interest rate in the bank. At the rate it was going they were concerned that their travel funds would come to an end one day, and they so looked forward to the annual jaunts.

They always looked for trips that allowed them to take Molly, their beloved dog, with them. They liked to take Molly to the dog park and let her romp with the other dogs. It was quite a distance from home to do this, or they would have taken her more often. When their local community was raising funds for their park, the wished they could support the effort.

Rita remembered listening to the man on the television commercial that was always talking about how his clients had not lost a dime in the stock market and were happy to have a reasonable rate of return on their money. She decided to check it out, and she found that she could not only guarantee a check for over $1600 every year, she could do this even after donating $2,500 for the community dog park.

The only problem was they had to cancel the CD at the bank and take an interest penalty to do so. But since interest rates were so low anyway, the penalty amounted to a pittance. Having just come back from their annual trip, they moved the money to the new account, and looked forward to the process of deciding their next adventure, knowing full well that they would have funds coming in to pay for it. They were not only receiving over 5% on their savings, they were guaranteed that there would be a check there for them for as long as they lived.

And now, while going over their memories from the last trip, they could go to the new dog park, and enjoy watching the dogs play while sitting on the new bench that had been named in their honor.

## LINDA

Like many seniors, Linda had seen many of her neighbors in need of health care, and how they had used up their savings in paying for care at home. While some were able to get by with home care, others had to go to a nursing facility. Many wound up having to rely on Medicaid, and that meant they were required to use up their savings in order to qualify.

Linda was not so much worried about the cost of nursing homes, as she had no desire to give them any business, and would much prefer to pay someone to provide care at home if needed. But the cost of home care is not cheap, either. She had money set aside specifically for the purpose of paying for home care if needed in the future.

The money she had saved was invested in a $75,000 CD at the bank, and she had made arrangements in her will to leave any balance in that account to her church. She would have donated it immediately, if she could, but it was her health care fund, and she did not know if it would be needed.

She was always looking for answers to the problem of low interest rates on her savings, and in her reading, she heard that some people were using life insurance plans. Instead of making payments on a policy, they were simply making a single deposit with the insurance company. Not only did they receive a higher interest rate on the savings, there was a valuable insurance benefit included.

Linda found that at the age of 65, her $75,000 account would give her a fully paid up life insurance plan in the amount of $125,000. Most importantly, she found that the full amount would be available for her use if she needed home care at any point in the future. And, if she named the church as the beneficiary, they would receive the entire account balance directly from the insurance company with no need to wait for the probate system to process her will.

By simply transferring her savings account to a different financial institution, she increased her health care fund by over 50%. For her, that was a significant 'right now' benefit for her peace of mind. Along with that came the potential for a much larger bequeath to her church if she did not need the money during her lifetime.

Linda was delighted with her decision to inform herself. Looking back, she wondered: 'How many others have left a bank account to the church in their will, and would have been able to substantially increase their legacy if only they had known?'

(This example demonstrates the efficacy of using the benefits and guarantees available from a specialized life insurance plan. While Linda was no longer protected by FDIC, she did understand that there was a backup guarantee plan provided to all insurance policyholders in her state.)

## LEONARD

After being self employed for so many years, Leonard was tired of paying so much for health insurance. And he was also tired of facing such high deductibles that he never seemed to meet.

So when he turned 65 and became eligible for Medicare, he was relieved to find that his medical coverage would be so much better in the future, and that all he had to pay for would be that part of the bills that Medicare did not cover.

He was approached by a large number of insurance sales people who offered to sell him plans to pay what Medicare failed to pay. He found that of all the plans, the one that did the best job was plan 'F', as that plan covered all the unpaid portions of doctors and hospital bills. He liked that he could use any doctor or hospital in the country with no prior approval. They just were required to accept Medicare. The prices for this plan all seemed to be around $2,000 a year, which seemed reasonable compared to what he had be accustomed to paying for medical coverage.

He was about ready to order the supplemental coverage when he received a call from another sales person whose offer made sense to him. If he would be willing to pay the first $2,100 every year, they would reduce his cost for plan 'F' by $1,500. He thought: Why on earth would I pay the insurance company an extra $1,500 a year to cover a possible $2,100 loss? Why had no other sales person offered this?

Leonard had been considering taking up an offer from his university for a gift annuity, and to him, this would be the perfect answer for him to avoid paying insurance premiums for as long as he lived. Since the premiums for the high deductible plan were under $500 a year, he checked to see how much a $20,000 deposit would guarantee every month. He was happy to see that not only would the university receive current funding of $10,000, they would send him $940 a year for the rest of his life. On top of it, he would receive a tax deduction currently for the charitable contribution in the amount of almost $6,500.

Leonard had the gift annuity payments made directly to his savings account at his credit union, and instructed the insurance company to withdraw the premiums from the same account. The extra amount was available to pay for any current payments due to doctors. That extra amount was over $500 a year and Leonard found that the average amount paid out by medigap plans for people his age was about $500 a year. He figured he was fully funded for the rest of his life with just a single deposit, and he got help from the IRS in the process when he took credit for his charitable deduction.

(This example shows how setting up a guaranteed income stream from a gift annuity can be used to support a charitable cause. It also can add to the peace of mind of the donor. Leonard not only did away with future insurance premiums, he enjoyed a head start toward meeting the annual deductible of his supplemental plan F. And, if he remained in good health, the amount not needed every year for routine bills would build his account for future use.)

## HARRIET

Harriet was living in a retirement community.   Having lost her husband, she was now forced to live on her social security check. She did have the proceeds of her husband's insurance policy in the amount of $150,000, which she had put in the bank.

The bank interest was low, but she was afraid to use the money for fear that she would run out of money before she died.  Her children were all grown and married, and they were doing well financially.  She had given some thought to leaving her bank account to charity, but she also wanted to help them out while she was still around to see the money at work.

After consulting with the charity, she was offered their gift annuity program.  By placing
$50,000 of her savings into a gift annuity, she was able to enjoy the income from it without wondering if the income would end before she died.

At her age, 70, she was able to have a regular monthly check from her gift annuity account.   That monthly payout was based on a payout a little over 5% of her $50,000 deposit.  That worked out to over $200 a month which was an immediate help to her quality of life.

While the tax deduction actually meant little to her, she was happy to be able to help her charity achieve their financial goals while she was still around to participate.

She still had $100,000 to invest after using the gift annuity.  The same adviser had mentioned that other church members had set up a deferred gift program using a single deposit life insurance program. Even at her age, it was possible to obtain coverage by answering a few questions about her health to a telephone interviewer. By simply moving the $100,000 to the insurance company, she would have a fully paid up policy for $128,000. She liked the fact that she could access the account if she needed money, but even more she liked the fact that it allowed her to use the face amount if she needed money for health care while she was still living.

In her situation, with the approval of her children, she arranged to leave the insurance proceeds to her church. They would be entitled to whatever balance remained from the original face amount after any advances for health care to Harriet while living.

(This example combines several contracts. One provides immediate benefits to both the donor and the charity. The other provides future benefits to the charity along with immediate benefit of added security to the donor from the increased funds available for possible health care needs.)

# PART TWO

## 'Win-Win Tomorrow'

There comes a point in life for many senior citizens when they recognize that they are really managing assets for the benefit of their heirs. This point is reached when they have resolved the problems of funding for unexpected health problems, and have also satisfied the question of having adequate lifetime income. There are many who have a need for health care planning, but have avoided doing so. Those folks can well benefit by the use of some of the plans described here.

Most of the larger charitable organizations are well prepared to offer what is referred to as 'planned giving' programs to their donor base. Experience shows that smaller charities are less active in this arena. They seem to rely on more of the immediate funding answers that are constantly presented over the phone, television, or postal media. We are thinking of the smaller organizations in our models presented here, but even the larger organizations may find some new ideas by examining the situations we present.

There is a high degree of skepticism in the world of philanthropy as regards the use or mechanics of various insurance contracts. No doubt this is a consequence of the general challenge of understanding insurance. Nevertheless, it is a fact that their use does open the door to meeting the goals of both charities and individual donors. The examples we show will make use of various types of insurance contracts. These examples are even more important when the financial world is one of high tax rates and low interest rates.

We have summarized the examples in a way to have the title pique the interest in such a way to cause a donor to explore further, and perhaps one example will turn out to be a model for further action. All examples will have in common the feeling of satisfaction to the individual donor along with the benefit for charity.

## SALLY

Sally's deceased husband had been managing a rental residence for a number of years that was located in a nice part of the city. He had bought it under favorable conditions, and had been fortunate in finding good tenants. But her husband was now passed on, and Sally did not want to be a landlord.

Howard, her husband, had left her with adequate life insurance, and along with social security, she did not really need the income that the rental provided. Even more so, she did not need the responsibility of looking after the rental home.

When she decided it was a good idea to sell the home, but she was shocked to find that she would need to pay taxes on the profit of over $200,000. She really thought it a shame to give all those tax dollars to the IRS when they could be used to help with the college education of her grandchildren. The home was on the market for $240,000, and the accountant told her that the 'cost basis' was just $25,000. After selling expenses were deducted, she would still have a taxable gain close to $200,000.

Every day, the mailman brought please for financial help, and most of them found their way to the waste basket, even though she was sympathetic to their needs. One day, at church, a friend of hers told how they had helped their tax bill by using a gift annuity offered by the church. She contacted the representative at the church, and explained her situation. He listened and made a suggestion.

"When you receive an offer for the purchase of that rental home, instruct the realtor to contact our office. We can do the legal work ahead of time so that, in effect, you donate the property to the church, and we will become the seller. As a church, we do not need to pay income tax on the sale. We can the take the full proceeds and apply them to a gift annuity contract for you to use for your education fund. We can arrange for it to pay out immediately, or we can defer it for a few years when the need for college funding starts. The capital gains tax on the profits from the rental home will be spread out over the next few years, making them much more manageable...

In the meantime, you will receive a tax 'credit' for the donation, and this credit can be used to offset the taxes on your other income, including the withdrawal of funds from your IRA when the IRS demands that you take annual withdrawals. At the age of 69, these mandatory withdrawals would start in a year for her.

Sally did not need the current income from her gift which was just over $11,000 a year, and was guaranteed to last for her lifetime. She elected to put these funds to work in a life insurance policy that would become fully paid up in 10 years. The amount of the insurance would be for $140,000, and after 10 years, the annual income would be available for any other purpose for as long as she lived. She liked the idea of using insurance as it provided a fund for her future health care needs if she was confined to her home or to a nursing facility. If she did not need this feature, the $140,000 would be available to her grandchildren for their college expenses when she passed on. Starting with the 11th year they would receive the income as long as she lived.

Instead of having a large tx bill to pay, the gift to her church resulted in an estimated tax deduction of $85,000 which could be spread out over the next few years if needed. It provided immediate funds to her church in excess of $110,000. She felt that Howard would be happy with the result from a real estate investment that he had made quite a few years earlier.

25

# FRANK

In the introduction to this book, we made reference to the billionaire that left his entire estate to his church. That meant that his family did not receive it. They also did not receive a bill for the federal estate tax of $500,000,000. What they did receive was the tax free proceeds of a life insurance policy. We do not know the amount of the insurance benefit. Suppose it could have been just $500,000,000, let's say. If you were a family member receiving those proceeds tax free, would you be upset?

Following the example of this well known billionaire, Frank was only a mere millionaire. And, at the age of 70, he really did not want to disinherit his own family. In other words, he wanted them to fully enjoy the fruits of his efforts over the years of his career as an attorney.

He also has a long held desire to help the university that had educated him. He was aware of their need for funds and in sympathy to their goals. An idea was presented to him by his planner that intrigued him. Why not leave his $500,000 IRA account to his university? They would be able to receive the full amount free of taxation.

Because he was well aware of the deferred taxes due on IRA accounts, Frank knew that there would be a big tax bill to be paid by his beneficiaries before they would receive the proceeds of his $500,000 account. Probably they would wind up with less than $350,000. He also knew that his university would be able to receive the full $500,000 tax free. It made sense to him to find a way to leave that IRA account to the university without disinheriting his own family

Instead of a formal trust, Frank just used the earnings distributions every year to buy a 'last survivor life insurance' plan that would pay off when both he and his wife had passed on – the exact time when his estate assets would go to his family beneficiaries.

When he priced out the cost of insurance, he found that he could obtain a policy with a benefit of $500,000 for a less than over $9,000 a year. Since that amount did not even use up the required minimum distribution for his account, Frank actually was able to have nearly $750,000 of coverage just by using the amount that he was supposed to withdraw every year.

Frank thought" "Gosh, I can more than double the value of my IRA as a tax free estate, and still leave the IRA to my old school! That's what I call putting tax dollars to work! Who wouldn't want to do that?"

## KEN AND KAREN

Ken is a 54-year-old executive at a large insurance agency. He purchased a vacation home a few years ago when prices were so low, thinking he and Karen, his wife, would make personal use of it when he could get away. It actually turned out that the vacation home largely sat vacant due to his busy schedule. It also turned out to be a good investment, as real estate prices had come back, and he could now sell it for a profit of over $100,000.

Ken and Karen decided to sell the vacation home this year and are looking for a way to offset the capital gain tax owed on the sale. Ken enjoys the challenge and responsibility of his job and is not quite ready to retire. But he is looking at planning options that will provide income in the future with the flexibility to retire when he is ready.

While Ken invested his energies at work, Karen spent years volunteering with their favorite charity and they wanted to find a way to make a special gift to help further its work this year.

They were both in good health and still enjoyed working. They were living comfortably on his current income, but were looking for ways to plan for retirement in the future. Ken wasn't quite certain when he would retire, so we wanted to find an income source that would permit him to be flexible with his retirement date.

A gift planner from their favorite charity told them that a flexible deferred gift annuity would help them meet their goals. Instead of selling their appreciated vacation home and paying high capital gain tax, they could give it to the charity and receive an immediate charitable tax deduction to offset their current tax bill. The flexible deferred gift annuity would permit them to elect to begin taking payments for life when Ken was ready to retire.

They decided to set up the flexible deferred gift annuity and were able to achieve all of their goals. They received a charitable tax deduction that year for the gift that was made and experienced immediate tax savings. When he is ready to retire, Ken will contact the charity to begin payments, giving him the flexibility to continue working as long as he wanted. In addition, the flexible deferred gift annuity makes it possible for them to receive a large portion of their future income tax free, and this was an attractive benefit to them!

(This story illustrates the flexibility that many gift annuities offer. Contrary to a popular notion, there is no requirement that the income from the annuity begin immediately. Indeed, many people use them as a future source of educational funding for the next generation.)

## JERRY

When he was ready to leave his job, Jerry was told that his group life insurance would lapse. He really did not need the coverage as he had lots of other coverage to protect his family. So, Jerry, who was about to retire at age 65 was about to let it just go. Since he had not been paying for it over the years, he had not paid much attention to it. He was aware of the fact that he could continue the coverage for himself if he paid the premiums, and there would be no questions asked about his health.

Jerry had other insurance in force, and had been offered to sell his group insurance to an investment firm. In spite of the attractive offer that he received, he did not like the idea of having some stranger own an insurance policy that paid off when he died.

Even though his health was not the best, he still felt no need to maintain the coverage as the premium to continue it would be rather high. Perhaps it was an angel that appeared to him after he heard the plea for funds at his church one Sunday. Or perhaps he just remembered the offer that was made for his friend's existing life policy. Either way, he came to evaluate the idea of making his church the beneficiary of that insurance, if he could just find a way to help the church with the premiums.

He talked it over with his adviser who suggested an investment that might just do the job. That particular investment was paying a dividend of over 8% annually, with dividends every month. He looked at the record of dividend payments over 5 years and also noticed that the investment had increased in value in spite of paying out those monthly dividends.

Jerry decided that he would transfer some of his savings to the recommended investment. It provided enough dividend income to his church to make the premium payments on the group life insurance continuance. The result was:

- Jerry was able to retain control of his principal
- The church was able to own the group life insurance
- Jerry took a tax credit for the annual dividends paid out to the church.

It was just a few years after that that Jerry passed away from a stroke. His family could still maintain the investment he had decided upon, and since the dividends were no longer needed to support the life insurance for the church, they were able to divert them to educational expense for Jerry's favorite grand child.

# GLORIA

If you have Required Minimum Distributions that are not required to sustain your lifestyle for retirement, you can turn those distributions into a substantial legacy for your favorite charity, no matter what happens to the economy or your investments.

There are no legal fees to do this as it is very simply employs using your own funds to purchase an insurance policy and naming the charity as the beneficiary. It makes no difference if you happen to use some of the face amount during your lifetime if you need health care. The charity is not the owner of the contract, just the beneficiary. They will get the entire face amount when you pass, less any 'accelerated benefit' you have needed to access. Here is an example:

Gloria had an inherited IRA that was her deceased husband's account that he had converted from an IRA. Its present value was around $90,000 but it was subject to swings in the stock market. She was not comfortable with that and did not really want to worry about it. She knew that she would soon have to take money from the account to satisfy the IRS, but did not really expect to use that money other than to reinvest somewhere.

So she simply exchanged that IRA account for one that had no stock market risk, and that promised her a known check every year for as long as she lived. At her age, 68, she qualified for a $100,000 life insurance policy for an annual premium of $4800

She took an immediate withdrawal of $4800 from the IRA to pay the first year premium, and authorized the IRA custodian to pay the premium from her IRA every year from then on. She never needed to worry about finding where to get the money to pay the insurance premium, nor did she care what the stock market would do as far as her IRA account.

She understood that the premium was guaranteed and that the

IRA payout was guaranteed to last for as long as she lived. She liked the fact that the insurance would pay an added benefit if she was in need of health care at home or in a nursing facility.

There was no cost to her from her budget other than the taxes she had to pay for taking funds from the IRA, but those were going to be necessary in future years even she did nothing about setting up the insurance. Also, the annual withdrawals helped satisfy the IRS requirement.

She named her charity as the beneficiary of the insurance policy, and the charity would receive not only the proceeds of the insurance, but also any remaining balance in her IRA account. By setting it up this way, she always had the option of changing the beneficiary, or even splitting up the ultimate benefit among several charities if she wished.

Gloria's example is one that shows how just a little forethought can make so much difference to worthwhile causes. Her immediate benefit was not limited to the good vibes from knowing that she had made a difference to her favorite cause. She had actually increased her resources if the event of a need for health care in the future, and by leaving the IRA to charity had effectively transferred the taxeson the account to her favoritye charity.

## JOHN

John is 69 years old and his wife is 68. John has a substantial account with his stock broker. He has one holding in particular that the broker thinks he should sell and take his profit since he feels the future for this holding is uncertain. The holding is presently worth $155,000, and if he sold it, John would be obliged to pay a large tax on a capital gain. His adviser gives him this idea:

Why not transfer $155,000 proceeds from the stock sale to a GIFT ANNUITY? By so doing, he would not only control the tax impact of the sale, he would help a charity that was important to him. If he sold the stock, he calculated that his proceeds after paying the capital gains tax would be around $130,000.  Instead of having a big capital gains tax to pay that year, he actually developed a charitable deduction of over $42,000

The gift annuity was set up to provide an income that would last as long as either he or his wife was living.  That income could then be used to fund ongoing payments for a life insurance policy that would leave money for educating his grandchildren.  It would be sufficient to pay the premiums for a last survivor life insurance premium with a face amount of $400,000

That is correct! You have just managed to transform a $155,000 gift (worth $130,000 after taxes) into a $400,000 benefit that he could dedicate to colleges expenses for grandchildren, or to pay the tax bill on the remaining IRA account.  You also have done the following -

- Benefited a favorite charity
- Eliminated the large tax bill for the current year
- Received a tax deduction for the current tax year instead.
- Created a significant educational fund to leave to grandchildren.

In the process, you have also eliminated the problem of paying for the insurance, since the check to pay the premium will be sent every month directly from the annuity to the insurance company. The funds are guaranteed to last for your lifetime, and the insurance costs are also guaranteed to never increase.

You may wish to split the program into two segments in order to benefit two separate
charities.  Here is the question for you:   As an investor, do you know of any other investment that would allow you to 'guarantee' a three for one return?

# MARK

At the age of 71, Mark found that he really did not need to use one of his IRA accounts to live on. Overall, he was required to take $7,000 currently to satisfy the tax bill imposed by the government. He had forgotten that these accounts had yet to pass through the tax gate, and now was looking at an increasing tax bill every year.

In deciding what to do with the required distribution, Mark talked it over with the adviser for his church stewardship committee. He pointed out to Mark that some folks in a similar position had actually taken out a life insurance plan and made the church the owner of it. By doing it that way, Mark would pay the premiums to the church and take a tax deduction for it, thereby offsetting the tax bill that he had to pay for taking the required IRA distribution.

Mark was somewhat dubious, since his health was not the greatest, but on further investigation, he learned that there was a way to use $6,000 of the IRA distribution to obtain $100,000 coverage. Since the plan was pay the face amount when both he and Mary passed on, his health condition did not become a problem. He particularly liked the idea that the plan would become fully paid up in 10 years, and that the distributions after that could be allocated to other uses.

There are many retirees in a situation similar to Mark. Not in need of the income, they look for ways to invest and find the choice to be either low interest bank accounts or risky stock market alternatives. The insurance choice lets them maximize the legacy to their church, and minimize their current tax bill.

(Mark was able to deduct the $6,000 gift of the premium to his church and that deduction along with the money left over from the required distribution allowed him to effectively leave his current tax bill unaffected by the mandatory distribution. The future benefit to the church of $100,000 from the insurance pleases both of them, and actually left the balance to his family. When he discovered the tax erosion that his family would incur, he actually took out an added insurance policy for the express purpose of paying the deferred taxes.)

## TONY

Like many people who saw their 401k balance reduced by over 50% in the market debacle in 2008, Tony was very leery about the stock market.  As a result, he changed the account over to a bank account with the result that there was no chance to recover his stock market losses.   As he sat on the sidelines watching, the market recovered gradually over several years.

He finally got tired of the low interest rates in his account and he talked to an adviser who told him there was a way for him to sleep nights and still receive high interest returns.  He found that there was an investment yielding over 8% with an extended track record of paying out dividends every month.  He had changed his account over just 2 years ago and it had now grown back to a value of $120,000.

Since Tony was not in the best of health, he felt that the account would end up going to his wife Tina who was in good health and whose life expectancy was well beyond his.  Tina would be in a good position financially with his pension going to her and also his social security check, so it was likely that the 401k account would pass along to his children.

In talking with a friend who he had worked with, he was told by his friend that if he left his account to charity, the full amount would go the charity with no taxes owed by them, and if he left it to his children, it would be fully taxable.  As a result, the value they received would be reduced by over 30%, possibly much more.

His friend decided to investigate how to avoid this big tax bite, and he elected to use life insurance as a substitute inheritance for his children. The amount they received would be tax free, and would be for a much higher amount.

Tony contacted his insurance agent who told him that because of his health, the premiums would be rather high. But for Tina, he could obtain a $400,000 policy by simply using a portion of the earnings he was receiving in his account which was now approaching $10,000 a year. If he lived 5 more years, he would be forced to start taking money out of the account anyway due to IRS rules known as the 'required minimum withdrawal'.

The policy he selected had a most valuable benefit that meant a great deal to both Tony and Tina. It allowed her to use money from the account if her health failed and she needed professional help at home, or in a nursing facility. She could actually receive up to $8,000 monthly if needed. Any amount not needed by Tina would be paid to her children when she died.

Tony thought: 'Gosh, here is a chance to regain some of those stock market losses, and at the same time contribute to my wife's financial security and peace of mind. The premium he selected was $9000 a year and that was easily handled by withdrawal from his 401k account, which had been changed to an IRA.

Since the insurance had multiplied the value of the account several times over, Tony felt completely comfortable in making arrangements to have the IRA account go to his favorite charity. So he made arrangements to have the IRA balance transferred at the time of Tina's passing when the earnings would no longer be needed to support the insurance premiums on her life.

In Tony's tax bracket, the actual cost of the insurance plan was just the taxes due on his $9,000 annual withdrawal, which in his case amount to less than $2,000 annually. He thought to himself – "I just turned a $120,000 account into a $520,000 account for my loved ones. And I am only out of pocket less than $2,000 a year, which the IRS will demand of me anyway in five years. Why doesn't everybody do this?"

# JIM and JENNY

At the age of 70, Jim woke up to the fact that his $300,000 IRA account was not 'tax free'. He became aware that he was required to take money out of the account every year, even if he did not need the money to live on. The IRS had waited long enough and wanted to start collecting their due.

Worse yet, he found that the entire account would become taxable at some point in the future when both he and Jenny passed on. His current account value was approximately $300,000 and if it became fully taxable today, the value would be reduced by nearly 40% before his children would receive it.

He could avoid this by converting the account to a Roth IRA account, but that would merely cause an immediate tax bill to be incurred. It did not make sense to them to incur this bill, but they did have to do something to satisfy the 'minimum required distribution' every year.

Here is what they elected to do:

- Transfer $200,000 to a separate IRA account that was guaranteed to send out an annual distribution in excess of $12,000. and they named their charity as the beneficiary for any account balance remaining in that IRA when they died.
- They also made the charity the beneficiary of the non transferred IRA account.
- They used the annual distribution from the new IRA account to pay for life insurance premiums on both their lives.
- The new life insurance would be for an amount of $450,000 with their children named as beneficiaries. The amount would increase as time went by, but would only be paid to their children when both of them had passed on.

The results of this program were as follows:

- The 'required minimum distribution' was satisfied for the foreseeable future.
- The charity benefited by receiving all IRA balances at death
- The family beneficiaries would receive the proceeds of the life insurance policy that was issued on Jim and Jenny. These would not be subject to income taxes.
- Taxes on all the IRA balances left to charity would be eliminated.

While this scenario is looked on as a 'win-win tomorrow' situation, there could also be a living benefit for Jim and Jenny. The insurance company they worked with had a provision to advance payment of the face amount if needed for health care expense – home care or long term care. This benefit would be available only to whichever spouse survived, and it was just an added benefit thrown into the plan which did provide some right 'now' peace of mind for both of them.

## DOROTHY

Dorothy had just become eligible for Medicare and had made a selection of a plan to cover medical bills that were not covered by Medicare. She was feeling much better about her financial situation now that the worry of medical bills was over. The only thing that still concerned her was the fact that Medicare did so little to cover the bills for home care or for nursing homes. In fact, her financial backup consisted only of a $100,000 bank account that was earning practically nothing.

She would have liked to leave something to her alma mater if she did not need the funds for health care but she did not want to disinherit her children in order to do so.

After going over her needs with her adviser, she decided to reposition her bank account into a separate investment that was paying out a tax free return of 6.5%. It was a bond account that invested in tax free bonds and it had a track record that was consistent. She was satisfied in her mind that it was a safe alternative for her nest egg.

That account opened the door for her to proceed to step two in her plan. She now had over $6,000 available every year to obtain an insurance plan that would increase her 'health care fund'. It was actually a form of life insurance. It paid off to her beneficiary even if she never needed money for health care. The plan that she qualified for was for a benefit limit of $250,000, and it would allow her to receive up to $10,000 a month if she were to need health care. Any amount not needed would go to her children free of taxation.

By going ahead with this program, she was able to leave $100,000 to her school in her will, and still leave a much greater inheritance to her children. All of this depended on her enjoying continued good health. Just in case her health failed, however, it meant a lot to know that there was a contingency fund of $250,000 available plus any remaining balance in her original account.

(Her planner suspected that the insurance fund would probably remain intact, as her children would be strongly motivated to take good care of her incase of illness. In any event, it was a great source of satisfaction to Dorothy that she would not be a burden to her children when her health failed.)

# EPILOGUE

The sample stories in this book all have in common a charitable mindset. They are simply a few variations on that theme. There is no limit to planning alternatives available.

There is an outstanding opportunity over the years ahead to transfer huge amounts to charity that would otherwise be sent to the IRS. We are referring to the trillions of dollars that are residing in 'tax deferred' accounts, such as IRA, 401ks, and even annuities.

The ability to make those tax dollars work directly for charity rather than being diluted by passing through various government bureaucracies can be accomplished entirely within the law. The only requirement is that some initial action be taken to educate the public, and we hope that this book helps to get the ball rolling in that direction.

## ABOUT THE AUTHOR

Robert J. Zimmerman brings over five decades of experience to the table in offering this book. On graduation with a BS in Finance from the University of Detroit, he served three years in the U.S. Air Force as a pilot. On separation from the military, he went back to the University of Detroit to obtain has M.B.A degree, while simultaneously entering the insurance business in Detroit at an agency started by his father.

He completed the requirements for Certified Financial Planner in 1982. He has also held a series 7 securities license, and has vivid memories of the market crash of 1987.

His orientation toward the guarantees of insurance contracts is a natural result of his years observing the vagaries of the stock markets, and he has a great appreciation for the idea of bringing sound financial strategies to those wishing to take full advantage of the 'age of information'.

He has published several books which are available from major online book stores, and are entitled:

THE ANNUITY – FROM MYSTERY TO MASTERY

THE MINI-MAX MONEY MANUAL

END MONEY WOND'RING

###

www.ingramcontent.com/pod-product-compliance
Lightning Source LLC
Chambersburg PA
CBHW070924180526
45168CB00005B/2145